ANCIENT CIVILIZATIONS

Ancient Chinese

by Tristan Boyer Binns

COMPASS POINT ... POLIS, MINNESOTA

First American edition published in 2007 by
Compass Point Books
3109 West 50th St., #115
Minneapolis, MN 55410

ANCIENT CHINESE
was produced by
David West Children's Books
7 Princeton Court
55 Felsham Road
London SW15 1AZ

Illustrator: Mike Taylor
Designer: Rob Shone
Editors: Kate Newport, Robert McConnell
Page Production: Ellen Schofield and Bobbie Nuytten
Content Adviser: Grant Hardy, Ph.D.,
    Chair and Professor,
    History Department,
    University of North Carolina at Asheville

Visit Compass Point Books on the Internet at
www.compasspointbooks.com
or e-mail your request to
custserv@compasspointbooks.com

Library of Congress Cataloging-in-Publication Data
Binns, Tristan Boyer, 1968-
    Ancient Chinese / by Tristan Boyer Binns.—1st American ed.
        p. cm.—(Ancient civilizations)
    Audience: Grade 4-6.
    Includes bibliographical references and index.
    ISBN 13: 978-0-7565-1647-5 (hardcover)
    ISBN 10: 0-7565-1647-1 (hardcover)
    ISBN 13: 978-0-7565-1954-4 (paperback)
    ISBN 10: 0-7565-1954-3 (paperback)
    1. China—Civilization—Juvenile literature. I. Title. II.
Series: Ancient civilizations (Minneapolis, Minn.)
DS721.B529 2006
951—dc22   2006002989

Contents

The Ancient Chinese

More than 2,000 years ago, Shi Huangdi started the Chinese empire. But ruling and uniting millions of people was not easy. Many later emperors struggled to keep it going. The ancient Chinese called their country All Under Heaven. The land was big enough to support all its people without any outside help. It was mostly cut off from the rest of the world. Although the ancient Chinese lived 2,000 years ago, we know a lot about their lives.

Look out for this man digging up interesting items from the past, like these ancient silver Chinese coins.

4

Who Were the Ancient Chinese?

China was made up of many states that fought each other. The first emperor united the states in 221 B.C., and many more dynasties followed. The first dynasty was called the Qin. It only lasted 14 years. The next dynasty, the Han, lasted 426 years. The final dynasty, the Qing, lasted 267 years, until 1911. Most dynasties were built upon the ideas of the previous ones.

Much of what we know about the ancient Chinese comes from their burials. The first emperor was buried with more than 7,000 terra-cotta soldiers. They looked like his real army. They were ready to protect him during the afterlife.

Because the Chinese empire covered such a great deal of land, the people spoke many languages and even looked very different. But the culture and traditions that bound them together into one empire grew stronger with each dynasty.

 More than 3,000 years ago, during the Shang dynasty, people used bronze pots to make offerings of food to their dead ancestors.

Liu Sheng was a Han prince. His tomb was made like his house, with stables, storerooms, and even a bathroom. His body was covered with more than 2,000 jade pieces to preserve it.

The Ancient Chinese World

Across China, people lived in various ways. Most lived near rivers because the land there is very fertile. It is also flat enough to farm. Much of China's land is high up or very steep and is difficult to farm. Most people made their living doing very hard work, such as farming and fishing. Some studied and became government officials. Many helped with major building projects, such as the Great Wall and the Grand Canal. The ancient Chinese believed they were at the center of the world. Even when they traded along the Silk Road, they thought they were more civilized than the other people they met.

A camel train

SILK ROAD (NORTH)

• Turpan

GOBI DESERT

SILK ROAD (SOUTH)

• Hotan

Himalayan Mountains

TIBET

The Ancient Chinese World

During the Qin dynasty, China was smaller than it is today. Its borders kept moving. At the time of the Qing dynasty, it was even bigger than it is now.

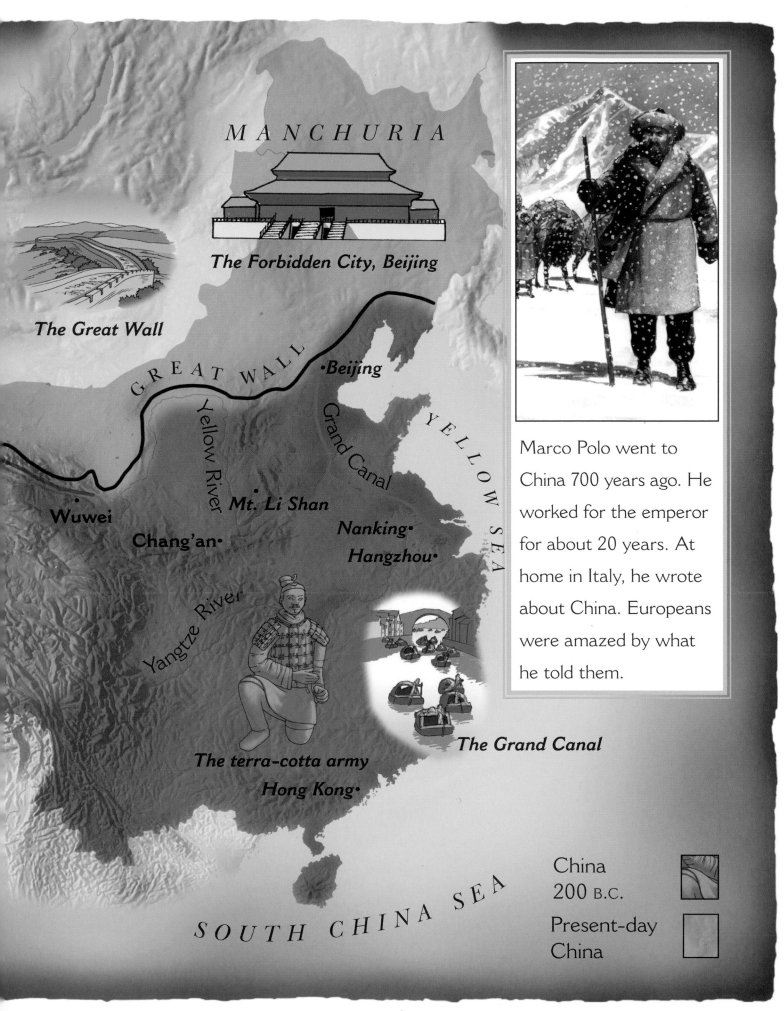

MANCHURIA

The Forbidden City, Beijing

The Great Wall

GREAT WALL

•Beijing

Yellow River

Grand Canal

YELLOW SEA

Wuwei

Mt. Li Shan

Chang'an•

Nanking•

Hangzhou•

Yangtze River

The terra-cotta army

The Grand Canal

Hong Kong•

SOUTH CHINA SEA

Marco Polo went to China 700 years ago. He worked for the emperor for about 20 years. At home in Italy, he wrote about China. Europeans were amazed by what he told them.

China 200 B.C.

Present-day China

Ruling China

Chinese governments had a clever system for keeping such a big land together. The emperor ran a large administration with officials in every part of the country. The emperor was called the Son of Heaven. He was the bridge between his people and the world of spirits. Not all emperors were good rulers. Some were cruel, and others were weak. When things went badly, people thought heaven had given up on the emperor. Then someone else could challenge the throne and even start a new dynasty.

All the emperors were men except for one, Wu Zhao. But women used their power as wives and mothers to help most of the emperors.

Chops are small stamps made from copper, jade, or stone. The end is carved in a kind of writing called seal script. It is pressed into red ink paste and stamped down. In China, people still use chops as their official seals.

It was very hard to get a job as a government official. It was a great honor. Boys could study for 10 years before taking the exam. At one point during the Song dynasty, there were more than 80,000 people taking the exam. Only one in 130 passed.

City Life

Ancient Chinese cities were busy places. People bought fresh food most days at the city markets. Children rushed around. Some were rich boys going to school. Others were acrobats, putting on shows to entertain people. All cities had boundaries or tall walls built around them, with gates that locked. There were also walls around most blocks inside the cities. These walls contained nobles' and officials' big courtyard houses and offices. Their solid houses and rich silk clothes showed their importance. The merchants and craft workers lived outside the walls. Sometimes their houses were built into the walls. All the farms were outside the cities.

A model of a noble's house made during the Han dynasty was buried in a tomb. The roof lifts off to show the inside. It has courtyards and a hall made ready for a feast.

Cities were planned to be in harmony with the heavens. Most were laid out in grids. A feng shui compass helped the planners put things in the right place.

During the Tang dynasty, the city of Chang'an was the largest in the world. More than a million people lived inside its walls, and another million lived outside. Many people came to trade in Chang'an.

Country Life

Farmers had to work hard all day. In the northern part of China, people grew wheat, and in the south they grew rice. Every possible bit of land was farmed. On land near hills, they built steps to stop the soil from falling down the slopes. The farmers paid taxes with a part of their crops. They also had to leave home and help build big projects, such as the Great Wall.

Making harvested grain ready to use took lots of work. A model shows a farmer using a machine to take the outer layer off the grain so it could be ground into flour.

Fishermen sometimes used trained birds to catch fish. A lamp drew the fish up near the surface. Then the bird would pounce and bring the fish to the boat. The bird had a collar on its neck to stop it from swallowing the fish.

Few children went to school. They learned to help their parents from a very young age. Peasants in the country wore thin, rough clothes. They stuffed paper and rags inside their clothes to keep warm.

Most of the work on the land was done by hand. People powered "endless chain" machines that carried water to the crops. Oxen helped plow. Pigs and chickens were raised for food.

Distant Lands

Many Chinese people traded in the street markets for food and items they needed. Markets were noisy and crowded, and everything they sold was made nearby. Luxury goods, such as jade, glass, linen, and pearls, came from faraway places. Merchants spent their lives taking Chinese goods such as silk, spices, and tea on the Silk Road to Europe. They traveled by camel across central Asia.

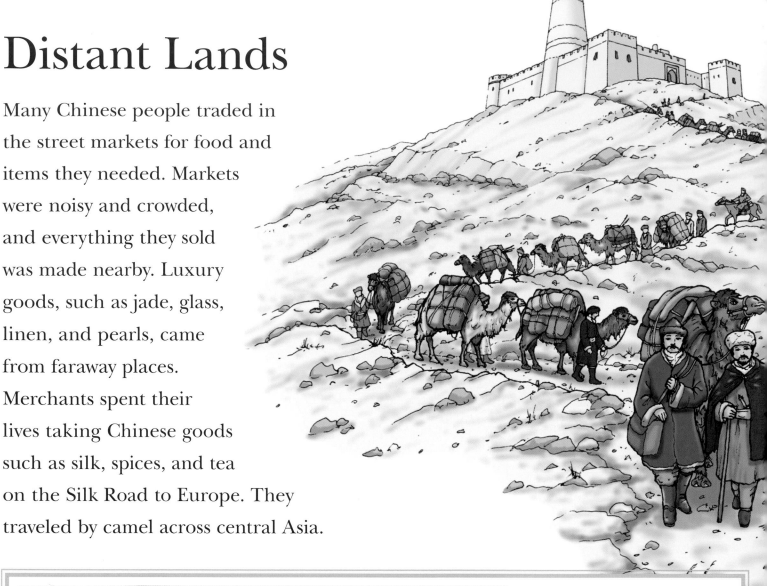

The secret of making silk from silkworm cocoons was first learned in China about 4,000 years ago. China kept the secret until about 1,500 years ago. Silk cloth from China was treasured as far away as Rome. Silk brought China money and fame.

The Silk Road worked so well because it was well guarded. Military posts and beacon towers helped keep trade caravans safe from attacks.

Early Chinese coins looked like tiny knives. The first emperor made the first round coins. They had holes in the middle so they could be strung together for safekeeping. Paper money was first printed 1,000 years ago.

The end of the Silk Road was 6,820 miles (10,900 kilometers) away, at the Mediterranean Sea. Merchants brought back goods such as Arabian horses with long legs that ran very fast. Ideas traveled along the trading routes, too. Buddhism came from India this way. The merchants were wealthy, but they were looked down on by other rich people and were taxed a great deal.

The Story of Mulan

Mulan pushed the shuttle through the loom as she wove the silk cloth. The shuttle fell silent as she began to sigh. She had seen the emperor's list of names. He was calling for soldiers to fight for him. Mulan's family name was on each of the 12 scrolls she had seen. But Mulan's father was too old to fight, and her brother was too young. Mulan stopped sighing and knew what she had to do. Mulan went to the markets and bought a fine horse. She dressed herself with armor as a soldier. Then she set off to join the fighting in her father's place. When she stopped for the

night, she didn't hear the familiar sounds of her parents calling her.

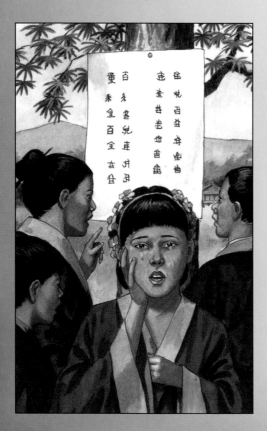

She heard the flowing water of a river that was far from home. The miles flew beneath her horse's hooves. The war unfolded. She fought in a hundred battles. Mulan lived as a man and was a fine soldier. When she was called to see the emperor, he wanted to reward her fine service. He offered her a high office or a rich prize. But Mulan only wanted a fast horse to ride back home.

When she saw her fellow soldiers again, they were amazed. They had never doubted she was a man during their 12 years fighting side by side. Mulan said, "Like with rabbits, there is not much to tell men and women apart. Running so close side by side, how could they tell?"

Mulan's parents greeted her with joy, leaning on each other for support. Her sister dressed up, and her brother made a feast in her honor. Mulan went to her room and put on her old dress. She made up her face and dressed her hair as a woman.

Beliefs and Festivals

Religious beliefs in ancient China were a mix of three main ideas. Daoism and Confucianism were strong at the time of the first emperor. Daoism is about harmony with nature and balance in life. Confucianism advocates strong families. The third, Buddhism, grew strong later.

For more than 2,000 years, New Year has been celebrated. Lions and dragons lead parades. Loud bands and firecrackers are used to scare off evil spirits.

Most ancient Chinese worshipped spirits in nature as well as their ancestors. Their festivals often celebrated the change of seasons. They were supposed to bring good luck. Even the hardworking peasants got time off. Lanterns, kites, moon cakes, races, and decorated boats were parts of various celebrations.

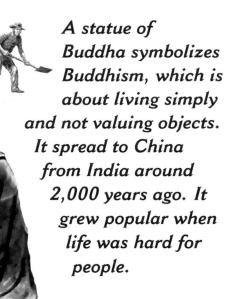

A statue of Buddha symbolizes Buddhism, which is about living simply and not valuing objects. It spread to China from India around 2,000 years ago. It grew popular when life was hard for people.

Confucius was born 200 years before the empire began. He believed that strong families made strong societies. He taught people to behave in the right way with their families and other people. Millions of Chinese have been raised with his ideas about respecting others.

Arts and Crafts

Artists and craft workers were important to the Chinese. Educated Chinese people all learned some of the arts as well. Instead of making words out of letters, the Chinese used symbols called characters. Each one stood for a whole word.

An artist paints a picture and uses calligraphy to add a poem alongside. The ancient Chinese thought that the way artists held the brushes and the way they drew the letters were as important as what was said and the way it looked.

To write well, a person had to learn thousands of characters. Then he or she used a brush to write them in a kind of painting called calligraphy. Other arts were also prized. Artists carved jade into sculptures, painted pictures of nature, wove colorful silk fabrics, and made delicate lacquer objects. Gardens that let people be still and think were also seen as works of art.

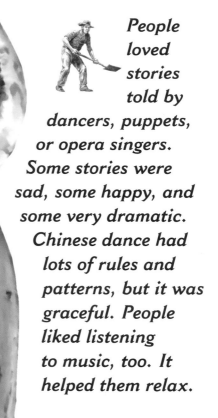

People loved stories told by dancers, puppets, or opera singers. Some stories were sad, some happy, and some very dramatic. Chinese dance had lots of rules and patterns, but it was graceful. People liked listening to music, too. It helped them relax.

The Chinese have used spinning wheels to make pots for more than 4,000 years. A special clay called porcelain was used to make thin, strong pots. They were decorated with tiny blue designs or bright colors. Chinese pottery was sold around the world. A Tang dynasty jug was made more than 1,000 years ago.

Chinese Inventions

The ancient Chinese used science and math to make their lives better. Dams and canals were built to stop rivers from flooding and to bring water to crops. The Chinese also invented the umbrella, the wheelbarrow, compasses, gunpowder, and paper. About 1,200 years ago, they also invented printing. This meant that more books could be made and more people could read them.

To make paper, shredded bark or cloth was soaked in tubs. A tray was dipped into the mixture. Its screen held a layer of mush. The screen was taken from the tray and pressed until the mush was dry. Each screen made one sheet of paper.

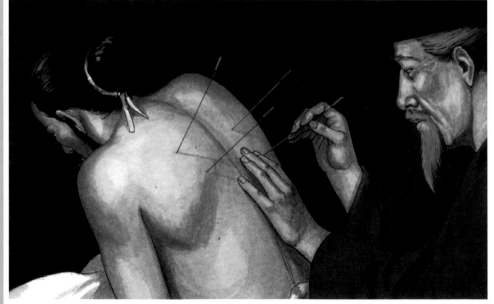

Chinese doctors thought that illness came from people's unbalanced body systems. Acupuncture used needles to unblock trapped energy in the body. Together with natural medicines, it could rebalance and cure a sick person.

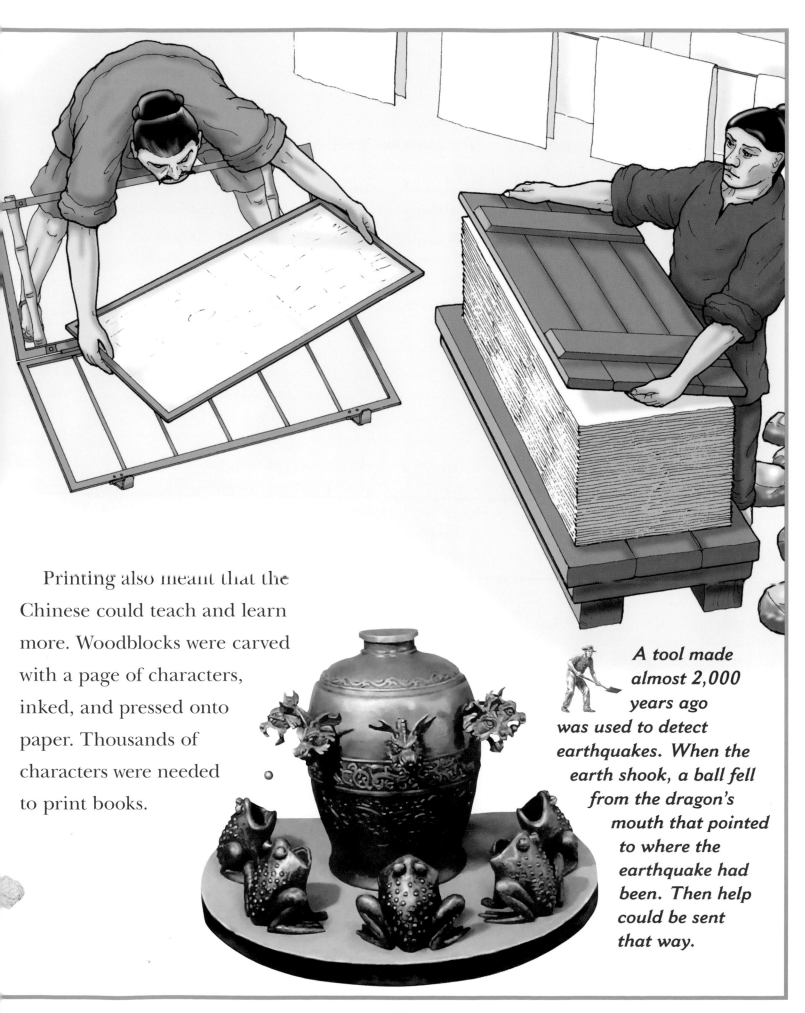

Printing also meant that the Chinese could teach and learn more. Woodblocks were carved with a page of characters, inked, and pressed onto paper. Thousands of characters were needed to print books.

A tool made almost 2,000 years ago was used to detect earthquakes. When the earth shook, a ball fell from the dragon's mouth that pointed to where the earthquake had been. Then help could be sent that way.

Great Building Works

Emperors often had grand plans for massive defenses, huge canal systems, or splendid palaces. They had three things that helped them build these great and lasting works. The first was building knowledge to make the designs strong and useful. The second was lots of artists to make things with beauty and harmony. The third was a vast work force that could be called upon whenever needed.

A lion statue is located in Beijing's walled Forbidden City. More than 200,000 men built the city about 600 years ago. It has streets, parks, and more than 9,000 rooms. Emperors lived in it for more than 500 years.

The 1,250-mile-long (2,000 km) Grand Canal linked the north with the rice-growing south. Boats were the best way to transport rice. It took more than 5 million men to build the canal 1,400 years ago.

During big projects, every grown man except for nobles and officials had to give a month's service each year. These great works helped every person involved feel proud to be Chinese.

The Great Wall was begun in 400 B.C., and it was worked on for more than 2,000 years. It helped protect China from northern invaders. Its 2,500 watchtowers could send messages a long way, too. Millions of men worked on it. It was such hard work that many died and were buried in the wall itself.

27

What Happened to the Ancient Chinese?

The last Chinese dynasty was called the Qing. At first, there were strong emperors. But around 200 years ago, the emperors stopped helping scientists and artists "discover" new ideas. They only wanted to follow the old ways and were out of touch with the modern world.

Hong Kong was an important harbor. It was won by the British in 1842. It grew into a rich and strong territory. In 1997, the British gave it back to the Chinese.

The last emperor was called Puyi. He was 3 years old when he took the throne, and he only ruled for three years. He lived in the Forbidden City until 1924. Later in his life, he became a gardener. He died in 1967.

Chairman Mao was the leader of a group that fought for poor peasants' rights. He won a civil war and ran China from 1949 to 1976. He was a powerful but cruel leader. He only allowed people to express beliefs that were the same as his own.

The Chinese people started to question the emperor's power as Son of Heaven. Britain, France, Russia, and Japan wanted to trade with China. Fights over land and the right to trade led to war. The empire lost power and land. In 1911, the Chinese people rose up against the emperor and made China into a republic. The empire was over.

Glossary

ancestor—someone in your family who was born before you

canal—a channel cut in the land to bring water to or from somewhere

culture—a group of people's beliefs, customs, and way of life

dynasty—rulers from one family who keep power for a long time

emperor—the ruler of an empire

empire—a large state made up of many countries, all ruled by a leader called an emperor

feng shui—the art of arranging surroundings to attract positive life energy

government—people in charge of running a city or a country

jade—a semiprecious green stone

nobles—people born into upper-class and powerful families

officials—people who help run a country or an empire

peasants—people born into families with little money or land

seal—a design printed in wax that is used as a signature

states—areas of land that have their own government

society—a group of people who have the same traditions and government

terra-cotta—a fired clay often used for statuettes and vases

trade—the buying and selling of goods such as jewelry and food

tradition—a group of people's longtime ways of doing things

Further Resources

AT THE LIBRARY

Kleeman, Terry, and Tracy Barrett. *The Ancient Chinese World*. New York: Oxford University Press, 2005.

Schomp, Virginia. *The Ancient Chinese*. New York: Franklin Watts, 2004.

Waterlow, Julia. *The Ancient Chinese*. New York: Thomson Learning, 1994.

ON THE WEB

For more information on the *Ancient Chinese,* use FactHound to track down Web sites related to this book.

1. Go to *www.facthound.com*
2. Type in this book ID: 0756516471
3. Click on the *Fetch It* button.

FactHound will find the best Web sites for you.

LOOK FOR MORE BOOKS IN THIS SERIES

ANCIENT EGYPTIANS
ISBN 0-7565-1645-5

ANCIENT GREEKS
ISBN 0-7565-1646-3

ANCIENT MAYA
ISBN 0-7565-1677-3

ANCIENT ROMANS
ISBN 0-7565-1644-7

THE AZTECS
ISBN 0-7565-1950-0

THE INCAS
ISBN 0-7565-1951-9

THE VIKINGS
ISBN 0-7565-1678-1

Index